NATIONAL GEOGRAPHIC
School Publishing

Inventions

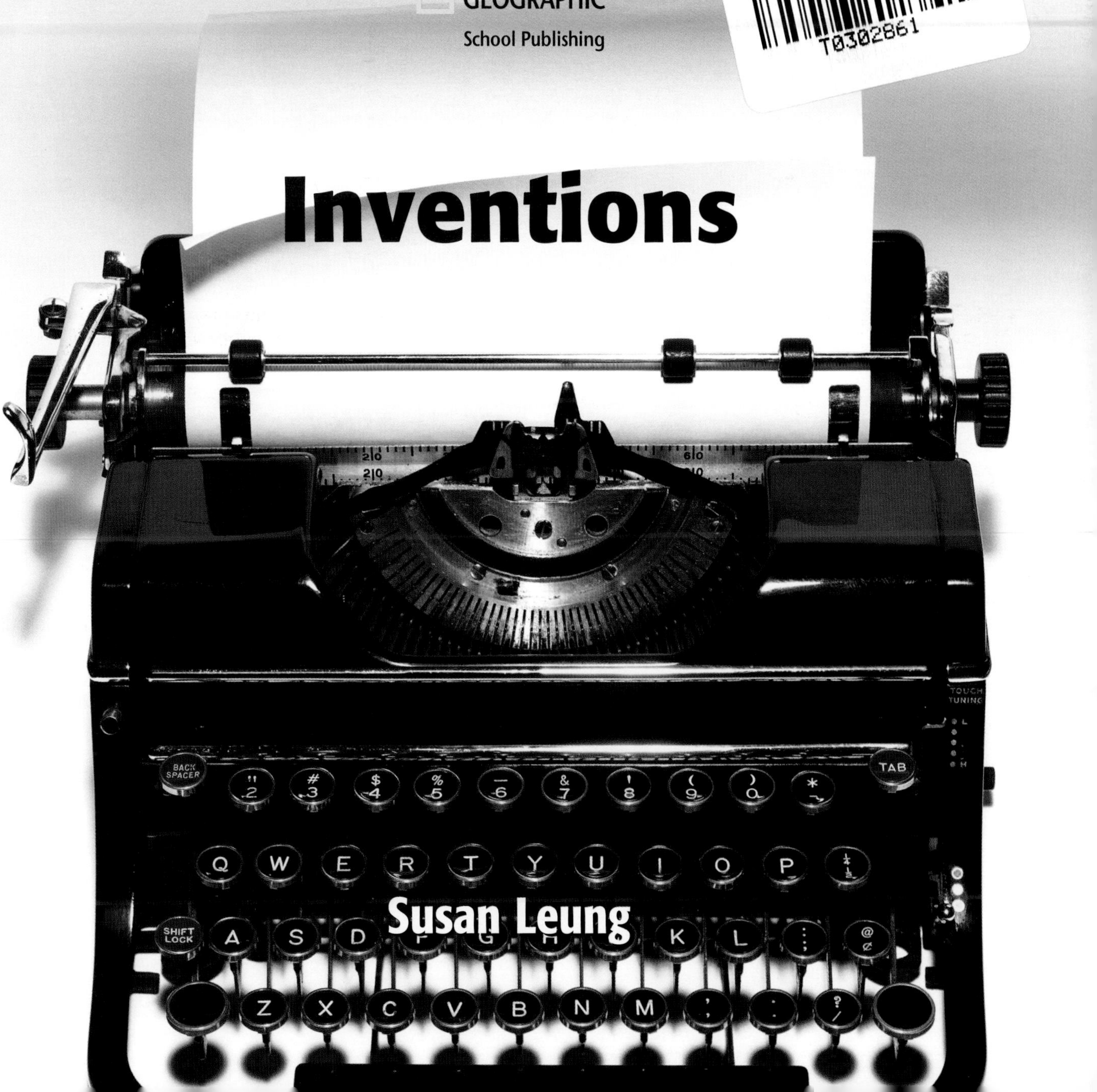

Susan Leung

PICTURE CREDITS
Cover, 1, 2, 4 (right above), 4 (right below), 6 (left), 7 (below), 8 (center), 11 (right), 13, 15 (below), 17, 18 (right), 19, 20 (right above), 21 (left below), Photolibrary.com; 4 (left), 10 (left), 10 (right), 11 (left), 11 (center), Comstock Images/Alamy; 5 (above), BananaStock/Alamy; 5 (below), 8 (left), 21 (right below), APL/Corbis; 6 (right), Dynamic Graphics Group/Creatas/Alamy; 7 (above), 15 (center), 16 (right), Getty Images; 8 (right), 9 (left), 9 (center), 20 (left), Gabe Palmer/Alamy; 9 (right), Medioimages/Alamy; 12 (left above), 12 (left below), 12 (right), 14 (above), 14 (left below), 14 (right below), Ibis for Kids Australia; 15 (above), Andriy Doriy/Alamy; 16 (left), POPPERFOTO/Alamy; 18 (left), WizData,inc./Alamy; 21 (above), Mark Jones/Alamy;

Produced through the worldwide resources of the National Geographic Society, John M. Fahey, Jr., President and Chief Executive Officer; Gilbert M. Grosvenor, Chairman of the Board; Nina D. Hoffman, Executive Vice President and President, Books and Education Publishing Group.

PREPARED BY NATIONAL GEOGRAPHIC SCHOOL PUBLISHING
Steve Mico, Executive Vice President and Publisher, Children's Books and Education Publishing Group; Marianne Hiland, Editor in Chief; Lynnette Brent, Executive Editor; Michael Murphy and Barbara Wood, Senior Editors; Nicole Rouse, Editor; Bea Jackson, Design Director; David Dumo, Art Director; Shanin Glenn, Designer; Margaret Sidlosky, Illustrations Director; Matt Wascavage, Manager of Publishing Services; Sean Philpotts, Production Manager.

MANUFACTURING AND QUALITY MANAGEMENT
Christopher A. Liedel, Chief Financial Officer; Phillip L. Schlosser, Vice President; Clifton M. Brown III, Director.

BOOK DEVELOPMENT
Ibis for Kids Australia Pty Limited.

Published by the National Geographic Society
1145 17th Street, N.W.
Washington, D.C. 20036-4688

Product No. 4W1005065

ISBN-13: 978-1-4263-5061-0
ISBN-10: 1-4263-5061-9

17 18 19 20 21 22 23
10 9 8 7 6 5 4 3

Printed in the USA.

Contents

Think and Discuss

What things do you see in these pictures? What was life like before they were invented?

What Is an Invention?

An **invention** is something new. It can be a new **product** or a new way of doing things. Inventions can change how people live.

This sewing machine was **invented** more than 100 years ago. People moved a foot pedal to make it work.

The electric sewing machine made sewing faster.

Long ago, people used kerosene lamps and candles.

The electric lightbulb provides light all night long.

Inventions and Change

Some inventions are **improved** over time. The telephone was invented in 1876. This **time line** shows how it has changed since then.

Alexander Graham Bell was an **inventor**. He invented the telephone.

Telephones did not have dials or numbers. An operator helped people make phone calls.

Telephones had a dial.

1876

1890s

1930

Cell phones became common.

The cordless phone became common.

Push-button number pads were introduced.

1960s

1980s

1990s

The phonograph is an invention that plays music. It was invented in 1877. Since then, new ways to play music have been invented.

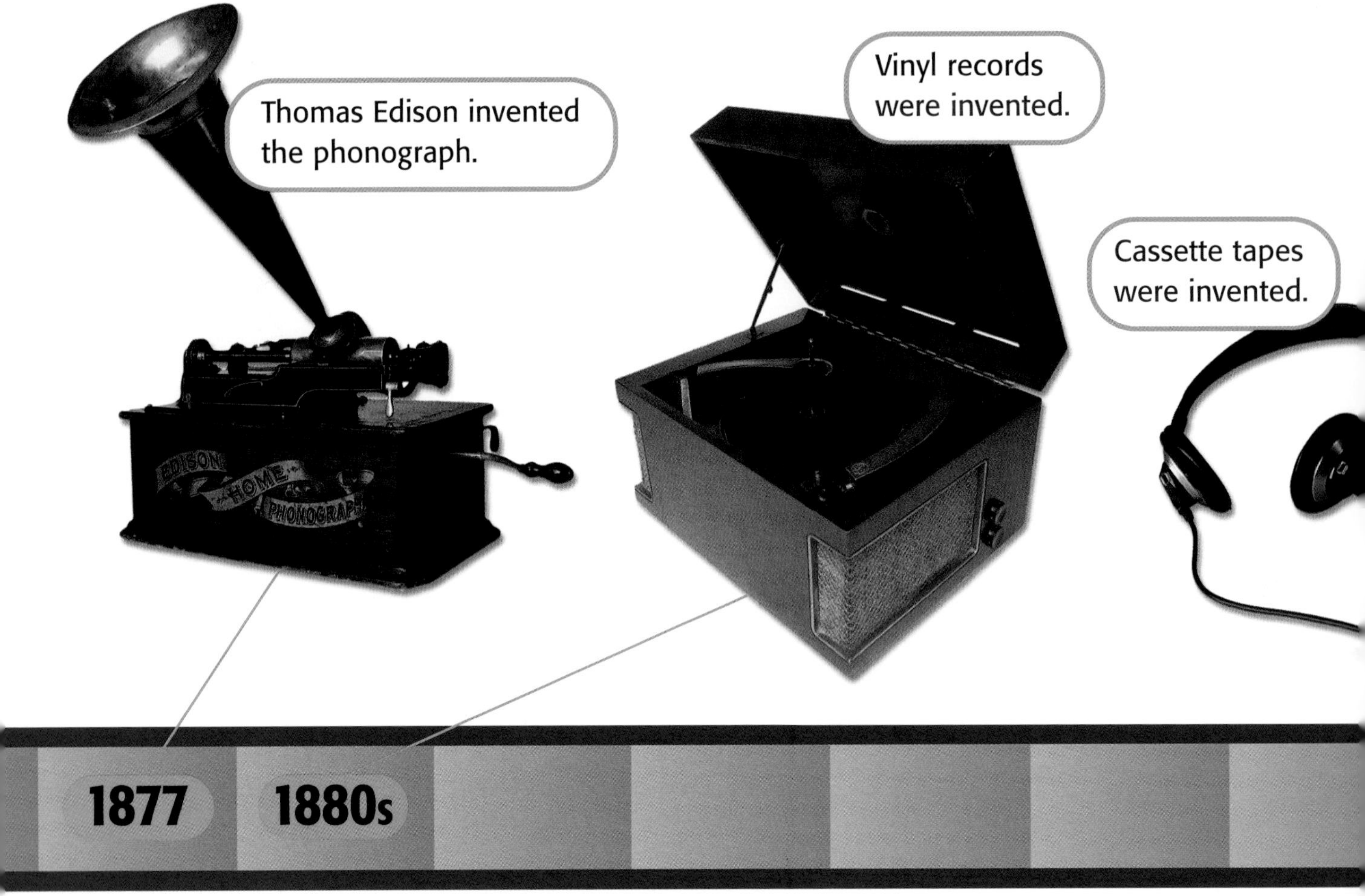

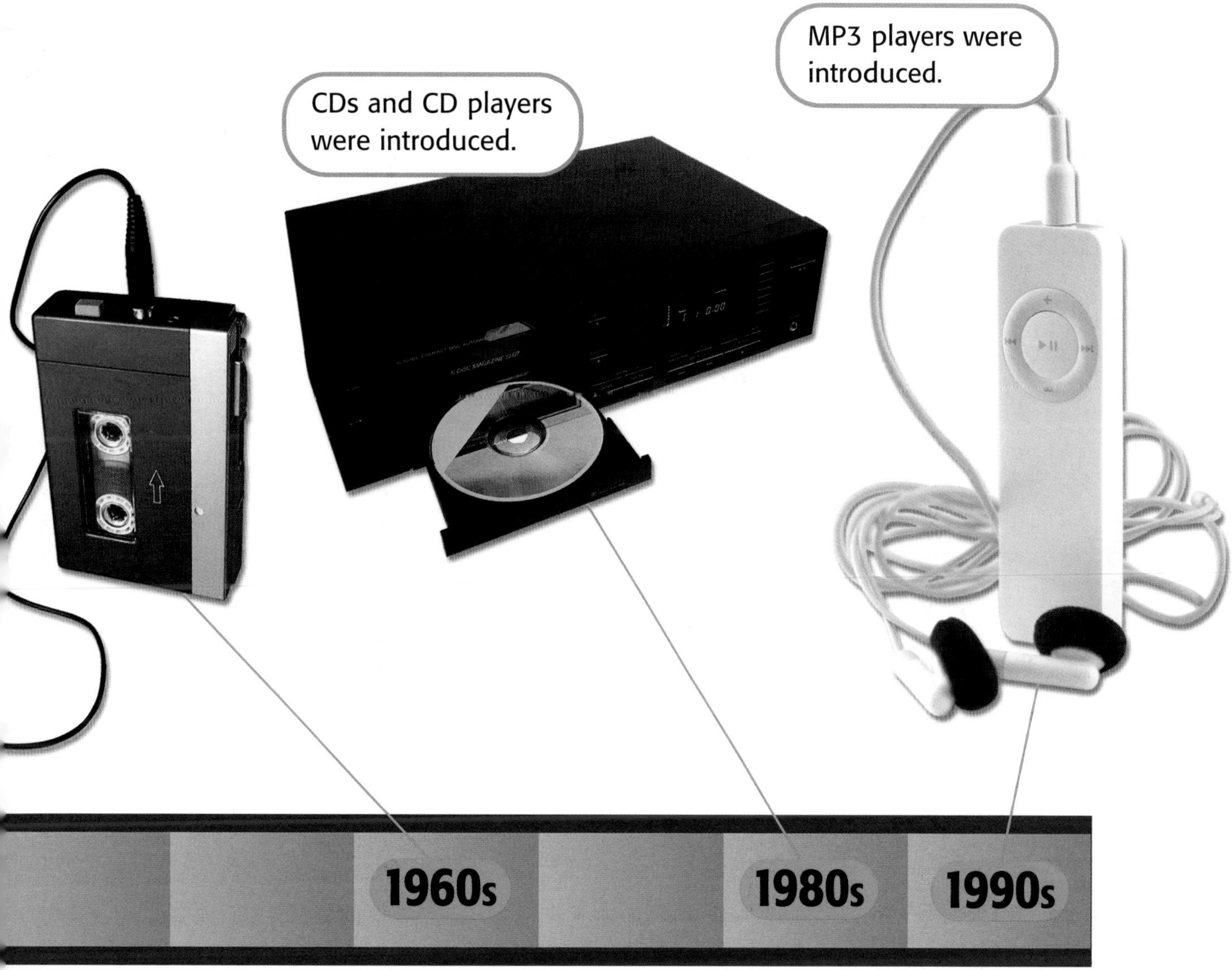
MP3 players were introduced.
CDs and CD players were introduced.
1960s
1980s
1990s

Staying the Same

Some inventions have not changed much over time. They are simple things. After they were invented, they did not need to be improved very much.

The safety pin was invented in 1849. Safety pins have not changed much since then.

Sticky notes were invented in the 1970s.

The paper clip was invented in 1899.

The sandwich was invented in 1762. It was named after the Earl of Sandwich.

Mayonnaise was invented by a French chef in 1756.

One Invention Leads to Another

Some products are used together. They were not always invented at the same time, though.

First the pencil was invented. Then erasers and pencil sharpeners were invented.

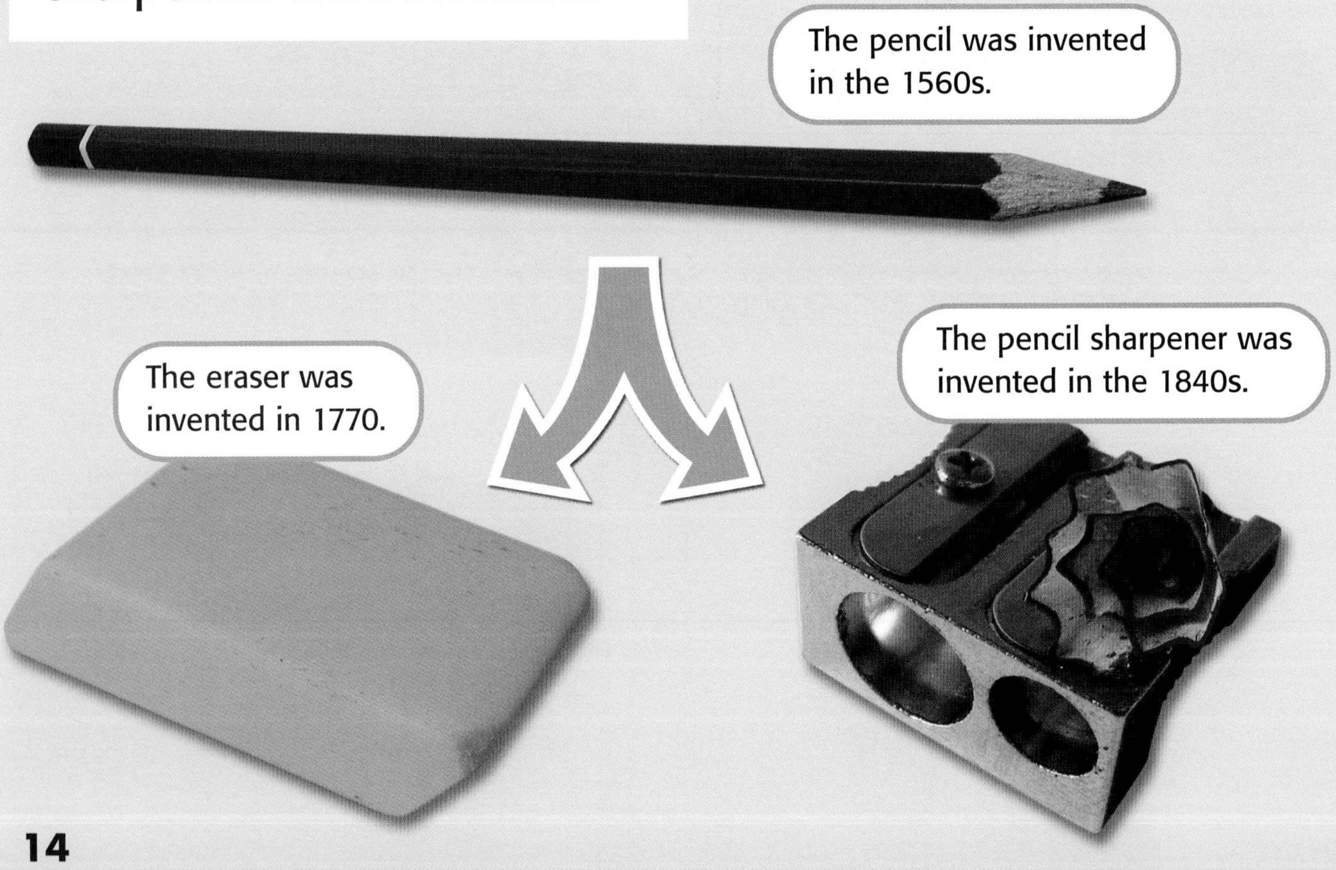

First the metal can was invented. Then can openers were invented.

The metal can was invented in 1810.

A special tool to open cans was invented 48 years later.

Today, can openers are quicker, easier, and safer to use.

Solving Problems

Many inventors solve problems. They invent new ways to help people. They might spend months or years solving a problem.

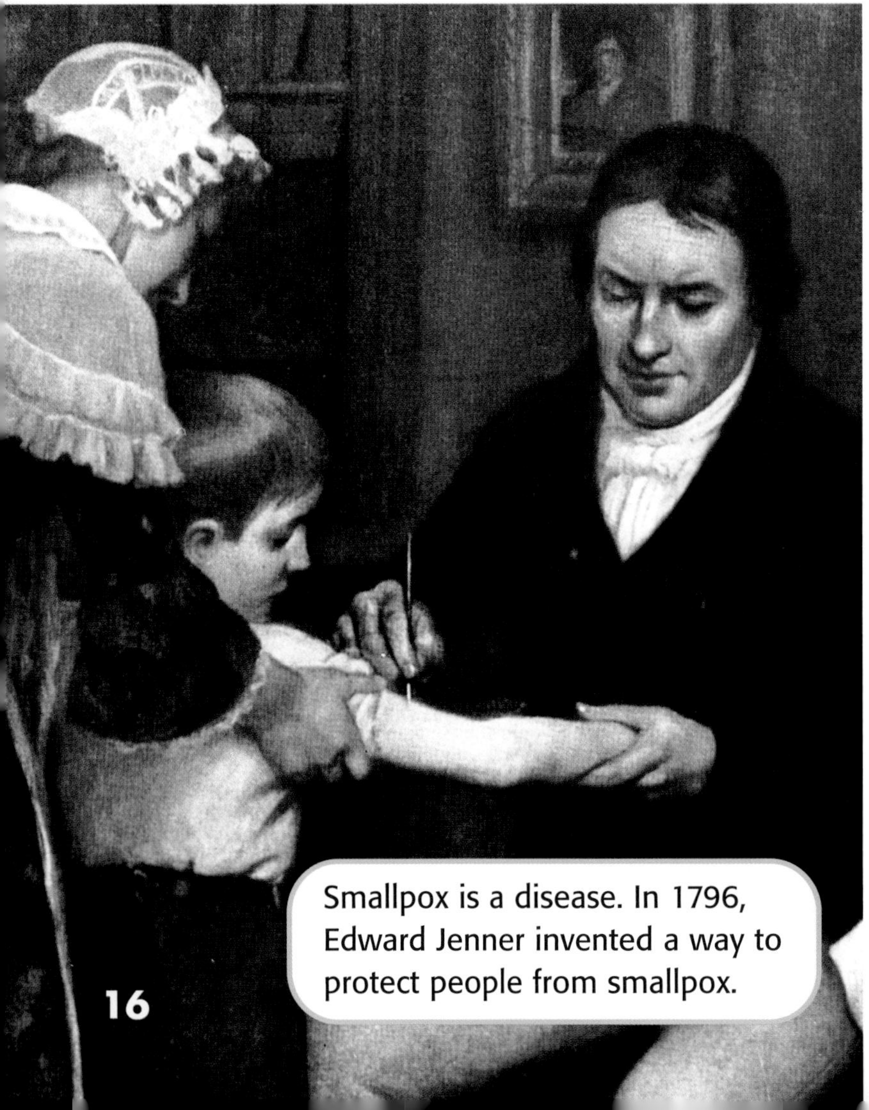

Smallpox is a disease. In 1796, Edward Jenner invented a way to protect people from smallpox.

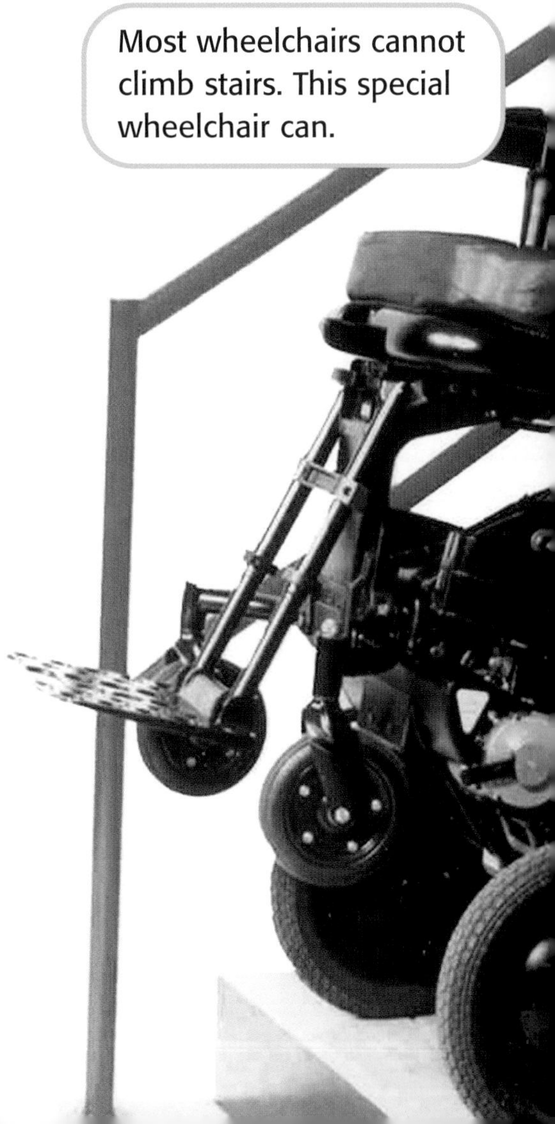

Most wheelchairs cannot climb stairs. This special wheelchair can.

In the 1820s, Louis Braille invented a way for blind people to read. This invention is called Braille.

Inventions We Wear

Some inventors make new things for us to wear. Even the fasteners on our clothes were invented.

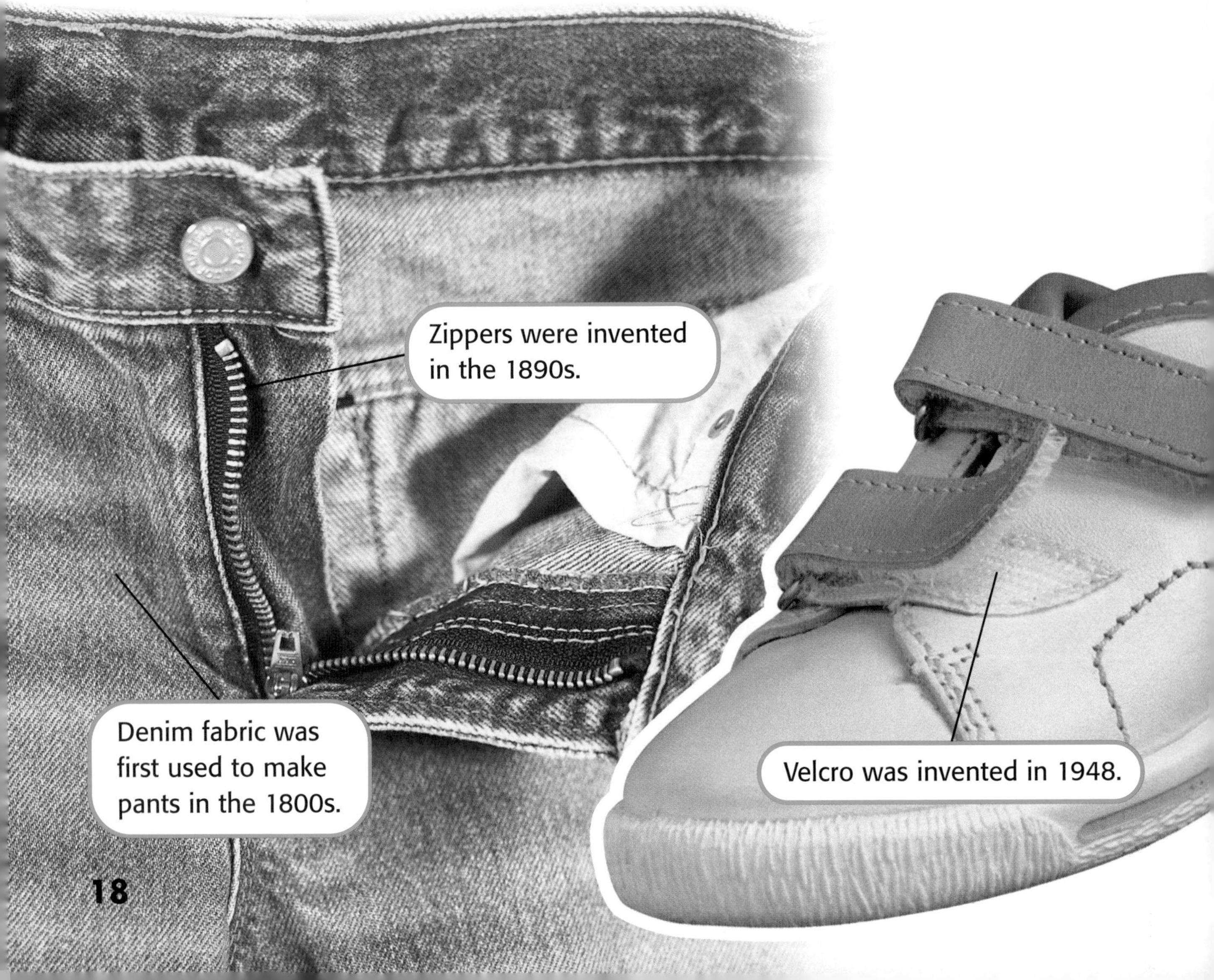

The first sunglasses were invented in 1752.

Stretchy fabric for sports clothes was invented in the 1950s.

Use What You Learned

How did these inventions change people's lives? How have they changed over time?

improve

invent

invention

inventor

product

time line

Glossary

KEY CONCEPT

improve (page 8)
To make something better
Some inventions are improved over time.

KEY CONCEPT

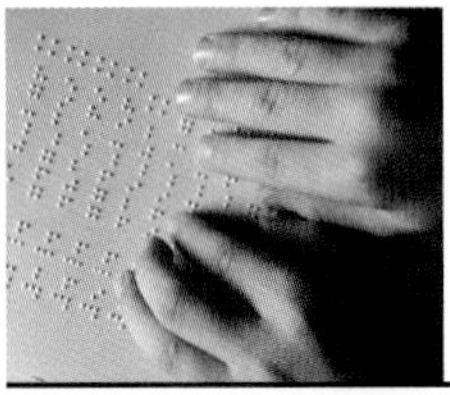

invent (page 6)
To create something that didn't exist before
Sometimes people invent things to solve problems.

KEY CONCEPT

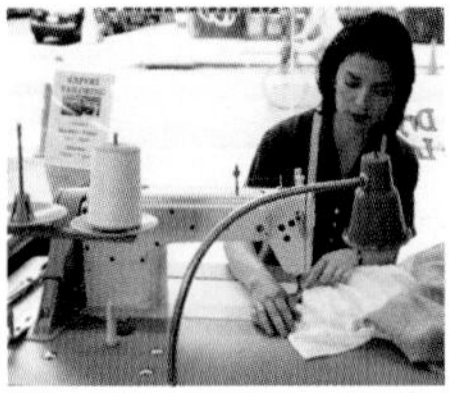

invention (page 6)
A new product or way of doing things
The sewing machine was a helpful invention.

KEY CONCEPT

inventor (page 8)
A person who invents something
Alexander Graham Bell was the inventor of the telephone.

KEY CONCEPT

product (page 6)
Something that is made for people to use
A pencil is a product.

KEY CONCEPT

time line (page 8)
A way of showing events in the order that they happened
A time line for the telephone shows how it has changed over time.

Index